NIST Special Publication 800-114

User's Guide to Securing External Devices for Telework and Remote Access

Recommendations of the National Institute of Standards and Technology

Karen Scarfone
Murugiah Souppaya

COMPUTER SECURITY

Computer Security Division
Information Technology Laboratory
National Institute of Standards and Technology
Gaithersburg, MD 20899-8930

November 2007

U.S. Department of Commerce

Carlos M. Gutierrez, Secretary

National Institute of Standards and Technology

James Turner, Acting Director

Reports on Computer Systems Technology

The Information Technology Laboratory (ITL) at the National Institute of Standards and Technology (NIST) promotes the U.S. economy and public welfare by providing technical leadership for the nation's measurement and standards infrastructure. ITL develops tests, test methods, reference data, proof of concept implementations, and technical analysis to advance the development and productive use of information technology. ITL's responsibilities include the development of technical, physical, administrative, and management standards and guidelines for the cost-effective security and privacy of sensitive unclassified information in Federal computer systems. This Special Publication 800-series reports on ITL's research, guidance, and outreach efforts in computer security and its collaborative activities with industry, government, and academic organizations.

Certain commercial entities, equipment, or materials may be identified in this document in order to describe an experimental procedure or concept adequately. Such identification is not intended to imply recommendation or endorsement by the National Institute of Standards and Technology, nor is it intended to imply that the entities, materials, or equipment are necessarily the best available for the purpose.

Acknowledgements

The authors, Karen Scarfone and Murugiah Souppaya of the National Institute of Standards and Technology (NIST), wish to thank their colleagues who reviewed drafts of this document and contributed to its technical content. The authors would like to acknowledge Tim Grance, Rick Kuhn, Elaine Barker, John Connor, Chris Enloe, and Jim St. Pierre of NIST; Derrick Dicoi and Victoria Thompson of Booz Allen Hamilton; and Paul Hoffman of the VPN Consortium for their keen and insightful assistance throughout the development of the document. The authors would also like to express their thanks to all the security experts that provided comments during the public comment period, particularly Miles Tracy of Federal Reserve Information Technology, Benjamin Halpert of Lockheed Martin, and representatives of the Department of State.

Note to Readers

This document was originally released for public comment as an update to NIST Special Publication (SP) 800-46, *Security for Telecommuting and Broadband Communications*. The scope of this document has evolved so that the document is intended to supplement SP 800-46, not replace it. As a result, the document has been assigned a different SP number.

Table of Contents

List of Appendices

Executive Summary

Many people *telework* (also known as *telecommuting*), which is the ability for an organization's employees and contractors to conduct work from locations other than the organization's facilities. Teleworkers use various devices, such as desktop and laptop computers, cell phones, and personal digital assistants (PDA), to read and send email, access Web sites, review and edit documents, and perform many other tasks. Most teleworkers use *remote access*, which is the ability of an organization's users to access its nonpublic computing resources from locations other than the organization's facilities. Organizations have many options for providing remote access, including virtual private networks, remote system control, and individual application access (e.g., Web-based email).

Telework devices can be divided into two categories: personal computers and consumer devices (e.g., cell phones, PDAs, video game systems). Each telework device is owned by the organization or an external entity, either a teleworker or a third party. This publication provides recommendations for securing external devices used for telework and remote access. Many organizations limit the types of external devices that can be used for remote access and which resources they can use, such as permitting teleworker-owned laptops to access a limited set of resources and permitting all other external devices to access Web-based email only. This allows organizations to limit the risk they incur from external devices. When a telework device uses remote access, it is essentially a logical extension of the organization's own network. Therefore, if the telework device is not secured properly, it poses additional risk to not only the information that the teleworker accesses but also the organization's other systems and networks. For example, a telework device infected with a worm could spread the worm through remote access to the organization's internal computers. Therefore, telework devices should be secured properly and have their security maintained regularly.

Before implementing any of the recommendations or suggestions in the guide, users should back up all data and verify the validity of the backups. Readers with little or no experience configuring personal computers, consumer devices, or home networks should seek assistance in applying the recommendations. Every telework device's existing configuration and environment is unique, so changing its configuration could have unforeseen consequences, including loss of data and loss of device or application functionality.

Implementing the following recommendations should help teleworkers improve the security of their telework devices. Some of the recommendations may be challenging for many users to implement, so users who are unsure of how to implement these recommendations should seek expert assistance.

Before teleworking, users should understand not only their organization's policies and requirements, but also appropriate ways of protecting the organization's information that they may access.

Sensitive information that is stored on or sent to or from external telework devices needs to be protected so that malicious parties can neither access nor alter information. An unauthorized release of sensitive information could damage the public's trust in an organization, jeopardize the mission of an organization, or harm individuals if their personal information has been released. Understanding how to protect such information accessed during teleworking can be confusing because there are many ways in which information can be protected. Examples include protecting the physical security of telework devices, encrypting files stored on devices, and ensuring that information stored on devices is backed up.

Teleworkers should ensure that all the devices on their wired and wireless home networks are properly secured, as well as the home networks themselves.

An important part of telework and remote access security is applying security measures to the personal computers (PC) and consumer devices using the same wired and wireless home networks to which the telework device normally connects. If any of these other devices become infected with malware or are otherwise compromised, they could attack the telework device or eavesdrop on its communications. Teleworkers should also be cautious about allowing others to place devices on the teleworkers' home networks, in case one of these devices is compromised.

Teleworkers should also apply security measures to the home networks to which their telework devices normally connect. One example of a security measure is using a broadband router or firewall appliance to prevent computers outside the home network from initiating communications with telework devices on the home network. Another example is ensuring that sensitive information transmitted over a wireless home network is adequately protected through strong encryption.

Teleworkers who use their own desktop or laptop PCs for telework should secure their operating systems and primary applications.

Securing a telework PC includes the following actions:

- Using a combination of security software, such as antivirus and antispyware software, personal firewalls, spam and Web content filtering, and popup blocking, to stop most attacks, particularly malware

- Restricting who can use the PC by having a separate standard user account for each person, assigning a password to each user account, using the standard user accounts for daily use, and protecting user sessions from unauthorized physical access

- Ensuring that updates are regularly applied to the operating system and primary applications, such as Web browsers, email clients, instant messaging clients, and security software

- Disabling unneeded networking features on the PC and configuring wireless networking securely

- Configuring primary applications to filter content and stop other activity that is likely to be malicious

- Installing and using only known and trusted software

- Configuring remote access software based on the organization's requirements and recommendations

- Maintaining the PC's security on an ongoing basis, such as changing passwords regularly and checking the status of security software periodically.

Teleworkers who use their own consumer devices for telework should secure them based on the security recommendations from the devices' manufacturers.

A wide variety of consumer devices exists, and security features available for these devices also vary widely. Some devices offer only a few basic features, whereas others offer sophisticated features similar to those offered by PCs. This does not necessarily imply that more security features are better; in fact, many devices offer more security features because the capabilities they provide (e.g., wireless networking, instant messaging) make them more susceptible to attack than devices without these capabilities. General recommendations for securing telework devices are as follows:

■ Limit access to the device, such as setting a personal identification number (PIN) or password and automatically locking a device after an idle period.

■ Disable networking capabilities, such as Bluetooth, except when they are needed.

■ Use additional security software, such as antivirus software and personal firewalls, if appropriate.

■ Ensure that security updates, if available, are acquired and installed at least monthly, preferably weekly.

■ Configure applications to support security (e.g., blocking activity that is likely to be malicious).

Teleworkers should consider the security state of a third-party device before using it for telework.

Teleworkers often want to perform remote access from third-party devices, such as checking email from a kiosk computer at a conference. However, teleworkers typically do not know if such devices have been secured properly or if they have been compromised. Consequently, a teleworker could use a third-party device infected with malware that steals information from users (e.g., passwords or email messages). Many organizations either forbid third-party devices to be used for remote access or permit only limited use, such as for Web-based email. Teleworkers should consider who is responsible for securing a third-party device and who can access the device before deciding whether or not to use it. Whenever possible, teleworkers should not use publicly accessible third-party devices for telework, and teleworkers should avoid using any third-party devices for performing sensitive functions or accessing sensitive information.

1. Introduction

1.1 Authority

The National Institute of Standards and Technology (NIST) developed this document in furtherance of its statutory responsibilities under the Federal Information Security Management Act (FISMA) of 2002, Public Law 107-347.

NIST is responsible for developing standards and guidelines, including minimum requirements, for providing adequate information security for all agency operations and assets; but such standards and guidelines shall not apply to national security systems. This guideline is consistent with the requirements of the Office of Management and Budget (OMB) Circular A-130, Section 8b(3), "Securing Agency Information Systems," as analyzed in A-130, Appendix IV: Analysis of Key Sections. Supplemental information is provided in A-130, Appendix III.

This guideline has been prepared for use by Federal agencies. It may be used by nongovernmental organizations on a voluntary basis and is not subject to copyright, though attribution is desired.

Nothing in this document should be taken to contradict standards and guidelines made mandatory and binding on Federal agencies by the Secretary of Commerce under statutory authority, nor should these guidelines be interpreted as altering or superseding the existing authorities of the Secretary of Commerce, Director of the OMB, or any other Federal official.

1.2 Purpose and Scope

This publication helps teleworkers secure the external devices they use for telework, such as personally owned and third-party privately owned desktop and laptop computers and consumer devices (e.g., cell phones, personal digital assistants [PDA]). The document focuses specifically on security for telework involving remote access to organizations' nonpublic computing resources. It provides practical, real-world recommendations for securing telework computers' operating systems (OS) and applications, as well as home networks that the computers use. It presents basic recommendations for securing consumer devices used for telework. The document also presents advice on protecting the information stored on telework computers and removable media. In addition, it provides tips on considering the security of a device owned by a third party before deciding whether it should be used for telework.

1.3 Audience

This document has been created primarily for teleworkers who are responsible for securing the external devices that they use for telework. The document also should be helpful to information security personnel and others who may need to assist teleworkers with their devices and remote access use.

1.4 Document Structure

The remainder of this document is organized into six major sections:

- Section 2 provides an overview of telework and remote access and an introduction to security concerns regarding telework devices.

- Section 3 provides guidance on securing information stored on or sent to or from external telework devices.

■ Section 4 presents recommendations for securing wired and wireless home networks used for telework.

■ Section 5 discusses securing personal computers (PC) that are used for telework through methods such as applying software updates and installing and configuring antivirus software and personal firewalls.

■ Section 6 gives an overview of securing consumer devices that are used for telework.

■ Section 7 discusses information that teleworkers should keep in mind before using a device secured by a third party, such as a computer provided for public use at a conference or hotel.

The document also contains several appendices with supporting material:

■ Appendix A presents additional security-related considerations for telework, such as using phone services (e.g., cellular phones, Voice over Internet Protocol [VoIP] services), using wireless personal area network (WPAN) technologies such as Bluetooth, using wireless broadband data cards, and ensuring the secure destruction of removable media and printed materials that might contain sensitive information.

■ Appendix B contains a glossary.

■ Appendix C contains a list of acronyms and abbreviations.

■ Appendix D lists print resources and online tools and resources that may be helpful references for securing telework devices.

■ Appendix E contains an index for the document.

This document is intended to be used by readers with various levels of experience and security knowledge, who are faced with different situations in securing their telework devices. For example, one reader might be securing a home network and a laptop, while another reader wants to secure a cell phone. Not all sections of this guide will apply to every situation.

2. Overview of Telework Technologies

Many people *telework* (also known as *telecommuting*), which is the ability for an organization's employees and contractors to perform work from locations other than the organization's facilities. Teleworkers use various devices, such as desktop and laptop computers, cell phones, and PDAs, to read and send email, access Web sites, review and edit documents, and perform many other tasks. Most teleworkers use *remote access*, which is the ability for an organization's users to access its nonpublic computing resources from locations other than the organization's facilities. For many years, dial-up modems were the primary communications mechanism for remote access, but their slow speeds severely limited what teleworkers could do. The increased availability of high-speed Internet connectivity has allowed for greatly expanded use of remote access.

This section of the publication provides an overview of telework technologies. It discusses commonly used remote access methods and talks about the need to secure telework devices, such as laptops and PDAs.

2.1 Remote Access Methods

Organizations have many options for providing remote access to their computing resources. The options most commonly used for teleworkers are as follows:

- **Virtual private network (VPN).** A VPN is a secure "tunnel" that connects the teleworker's computer to the organization's network. Once the tunnel has been established, the teleworker can access many of the organization's computing resources through the tunnel. The types of VPNs most commonly used for teleworking are as follows:

  - **Internet Protocol Security (IPsec) VPN.** An IPsec VPN can give teleworkers access to many different types of resources, such as applications, file servers, and printers. Using an IPsec VPN requires IPsec client software to be installed and configured on each telework device. Various applications, such as a word processor for viewing and editing documents, also may need to be installed. Because of the software installation and configuration needs, IPsec VPNs are most often accessed from computers issued and controlled by the organization. Some organizations permit teleworkers to install IPsec VPN clients on their own PCs. The client software is often preconfigured by the organization and provided to the teleworkers; otherwise, teleworkers can configure IPsec VPN clients built into their PCs or acquire, install, and configure third-party clients.

  - **Secure Sockets Layer (SSL) VPN.** Some SSL VPNs primarily provide access to Web-based applications through standard Web browsers. Other SSL VPNs are very similar to IPsec VPNs and can provide access to many types of applications; these types of VPNs typically require users to install additional software.

- **Remote system control.** Remote system control allows a teleworker to remotely use a computer at the organization from a telework computer. The remote computer has the software installed that the teleworker needs to run, such as office productivity software (e.g., word processors, spreadsheet programs) and organization-specific applications. The remote system control method most commonly used for telework is terminal server access, which gives each teleworker access to a separate standard virtual desktop.[1] Terminal server access requires the teleworker to either install a

---

[1] A less commonly used method is remote desktop access, which gives a teleworker access to a particular actual desktop at the organization, most often the user's own computer at the organization's office. Solutions involving remote desktop access can be more difficult to secure and maintain than solutions based on terminal server access (for example, exposing

special client application on the telework computer or use a Web-based interface, often with a browser plug-in or other additional software that the organization provides.

- **Individual application access.** A teleworker can access an individual application remotely, usually a Web-based application such as email access. This type of access typically requires only a Web browser on the telework device, so in most cases there is no need to reconfigure the device or install software on it before accessing the applications.

There are many ways in which teleworkers gain access to the Internet, including broadband networks (e.g., cable modem, digital subscriber line [DSL], satellite, and wireless broadband), wireless hotspots, other organizations' networks, and dial-up access to Internet service providers (ISP). For this publication, the access method used is typically irrelevant; any special considerations related to a particular method are highlighted.

Some organizations have pools of modems that teleworkers can dial into to directly access the organization's computing resources, instead of accessing the resources over the Internet. For example, an organization might have a toll-free number that users on travel can call from their laptops to get access to email. As high-speed Internet access has become widely available, the need for organization-hosted modem pools has decreased.

Most of the computing resources used through remote access are available only to an organization's users. Before accessing such resources, the users need to demonstrate their identities, such as with usernames and passwords. Many remote access solutions require teleworkers to authenticate multiple times; for example, a teleworker might need to authenticate to use a VPN, and then authenticate to individual applications accessed through the VPN. Many organizations have separate authentication systems for remote access, and it is common for teleworkers to be issued a hardware token and to have to enter a code from the token into the computer to be authenticated. Many organizations also require teleworkers to reauthenticate periodically during long remote access sessions, such as after each 4 hours of a session or after 30 minutes of idle time. These authentication options help organizations confirm that the person using remote access is authorized to do so.

Most remote access technologies and many individual applications are able to encrypt their communications automatically. This ability prevents attackers on the Internet and other networks from eavesdropping on the communications or tampering with them. It is outside the scope of this publication to provide a detailed explanation of communications protection. Teleworkers should check with their organizations as to what protection is applied to their communications, so that they do not inadvertently transfer sensitive information over networks without adequate protection.

2.2 Telework Devices

Telework devices can be divided into two categories:

- **Personal computers (PC),** which are desktop and laptop computers running standard PC OSs (e.g., Windows, Linux/UNIX, Mac OS). PCs can be used for any of the remote access methods described in Section 2.1.

- **Consumer devices,** which are small, usually mobile computers that do not run standard PC OSs. Examples of consumer devices are networking-capable PDAs, cell phones, and video game systems.[2]

---

internal desktops to malware from external devices), so many organizations do not permit remote desktop access from telework devices not controlled by the organization.

[2] Technically, some video game systems do run standard PC operating systems, but these are often hidden and are not intended for users to use directly.

Consumer devices are most often used for remote access methods that use Web browsers, primarily SSL VPNs and individual Web application access.

Where applicable, this publication provides recommendations specific to securing PCs or consumer devices. Another set of categories used in the recommendations is the party that owns the telework device. These categories are as follows:

- **Organization devices.** Telework devices in this category are usually owned, configured, and managed by the organization. These devices can be used for any of the organization's remote access methods.

- **Teleworker devices.** These are owned by the teleworker, who is ultimately responsible for securing them and maintaining their security. These devices can usually be used for many or all of the organization's remote access methods.

- **Third party devices.** These are owned, configured, and secured by third parties, such as kiosk computers at hotels, and PCs or consumer devices owned by friends and family. Remote access options for third party-secured devices are typically quite limited because users are often unable to install software onto them, such as VPN software, terminal server software, and Web browser plug-ins.

For various reasons, including security policies and technology limitations, organizations often limit which types of devices can be used for remote access. For example, an organization might permit only organization PCs to be used. Some organizations have tiered access levels, such as allowing organization PCs to access many resources, teleworker-owned PCs to access a more limited set of resources, and consumer devices and third-party PCs to access only one or two resources, such as Web-based email. This allows an organization to limit the risk it incurs by permitting the most-controlled devices to have the most access and the least-controlled devices to have minimal access. **Before using remote access, each teleworker should check with his or her organization to confirm that the organization permits the teleworker's PCs and/or consumer devices to be used for remote access.** Teleworkers should also be aware that many organizations periodically reassess their policies for telework devices and may change which types of devices are permitted, so teleworkers should ensure they review current information on remote access devices.

2.3   Telework Device Security Overview

In today's computing environment, there are many threats to telework devices. These threats are posed by people with many different motivations, including causing mischief and disruption, and committing identity theft and other forms of fraud. Teleworkers can increase their devices' security to provide better protection against these threats. The primary threat against most telework devices is malware. *Malware*, also known as *malicious code*, refers to a computer program that is covertly placed onto a computing device with the intent of compromising the confidentiality, integrity, or availability of the device's data, applications, or OS. Common types of malware threats include viruses, worms, malicious mobile code, Trojan horses, rootkits, and spyware.[3] Malware threats can infect devices through many means, including email, Web sites, file downloads and file sharing, peer-to-peer software, and instant messaging. Another common threat against telework devices is the loss or theft of the device. Someone with physical access to a device has many options for attempting to view the information stored on it.

Security protections, also known as *security controls*, are measures against threats that are intended to compensate for the device's security weaknesses, also known as *vulnerabilities*. Threats attempt to take

---

[3]   More information on malware is available in Section 5.4.1.

advantage of these vulnerabilities. Some vulnerabilities can be eliminated through security protections, such as a feature in an application that automatically downloads and installs new versions of the application that have corrected previous errors. For vulnerabilities that cannot be eliminated, security protections can prevent attacks from taking advantage of them, such as antivirus software stopping an infected email from being opened by a user, or hard drive encryption making files unreadable by others. Regardless of how many security protections are used, it is simply impossible to provide 100-percent protection against attacks because of the complexity of computing. A more realistic goal is to use security protections to give attackers as few opportunities as feasible to gain access to a device or to damage the device's software or information.

For an organization, permitting teleworkers to remotely access its computing resources gives attackers additional opportunities to breach the organization's security. When a telework device uses remote access, it is essentially an extension of the organization's own network. Therefore, if the telework device is not secured properly, it poses additional risk not only to the information that the teleworker accesses, but also to the organization's other systems and networks. For example, a telework device infected with a worm could spread it through remote access to the organization's internal computers. Therefore, telework devices should be secured properly and have their security maintained regularly.

Many organizations automatically check the security health of each telework device that attempts to use remote access to ensure that it complies with the organization's policies. Examples of the checks are verifying that the OS is fully patched, antivirus software is installed and up-to-date, and a personal firewall is enabled. Some remote access solutions can also determine if the device has been secured by the organization and what type of device it is (e.g., desktop/laptop, PDA, video game system). Based on the results of these checks, the organization can determine whether the device should be permitted to use remote access.

The remainder of this publication provides recommendations for securing telework devices. The recommendations address securing PCs and consumer devices, securing the networks that telework devices use, and protecting information stored on and sent to and from telework devices. This publication also provides guidance on evaluating the security of third party-owned devices, so that teleworkers can decide whether the devices should be used for remote access.

3. Securing Information

Sensitive information, such as personally identifiable information (PII) (e.g., personnel records, medical records, financial records),[4] that is stored on or sent to or from telework devices needs to be protected so that malicious parties cannot access or alter it. An unauthorized release of sensitive information could damage the public's trust in an organization, jeopardize the organization's mission, or harm individuals if their personal information has been released.

Before teleworking, users should understand their organization's policies and requirements and the appropriate ways of protecting the organization's information. This can be confusing because there are many ways in which information can be protected. Examples of methods that organizations may expect or require teleworkers to use are as follows:

- **Using physical security controls** for telework devices and removable media. For example, an organization might require that laptops be physically secured using cable locks when used in hotels, conferences, and other locations where third parties could easily gain physical access to the devices. Organizations may also have physical security requirements for papers and other non-computer media that contain sensitive information and are taken outside the organization's facilities.

- **Encrypting files stored on telework devices and removable media** such as CDs and flash drives. This prevents attackers from readily gaining access to information in the files. Many options exist for protecting files, including encrypting individual files or folders, volumes, and hard drives. Generally, using an encryption method to protect files also requires the use of an authentication mechanism (e.g., password) to decrypt the files when needed.

- **Ensuring that information stored on telework devices is backed up.** If something adverse happens to a device, such as a hardware, software, or power failure or a natural disaster, the information on the device will be lost unless it has been backed up to another device or removable media. Some organizations permit teleworkers to back up their local files to a centralized system (e.g., through VPN remote access), whereas other organizations recommend that their teleworkers perform local backups (e.g., burning CDs, copying files onto removable media). Teleworkers should perform backups, following their organizations' guidelines, and verify that the backups are valid and complete.[5] It is important that backups on removable media be secured at least as well as the device that they backed up. For example, if a computer is stored in a locked room, then the media also should be in a secured location; if a computer stores its data encrypted, then the backups of that data should also be encrypted.

- **Ensuring that information is destroyed when it is no longer needed.** For example, the organization's files should be removed from a computer scheduled to be retired or a third-party

---

[4] OMB Memorandum 06-19, *Reporting Incidents Involving Personally Identifiable Information and Incorporating the Cost for Security in Agency Information Technology Investments,* defines PII as "any information about an individual maintained by an agency, including, but not limited to, education, financial transactions, medical history, and criminal or employment history and information which can be used to distinguish or trace an individual's identity, such as their name, social security number, date and place of birth, mother's maiden name, biometric records, etc., including any other personal information which is linked or linkable to an individual." The full text of the memorandum is available at http://www.whitehouse.gov/omb/memoranda/fy2006/m-06-19.pdf.

[5] If the backups are not valid or complete, information may be lost, so validation of backups is very important. Some backup utilities offer features that can check each backup to ensure it is valid. For a simple backup, such as copying files to removable media, a teleworker may be able to check the backup by opening a sampling of files from the media. Teleworkers can also test the backup restoration process, such as restoring a backup onto another computer or restoring backed-up files into a separate test folder. Teleworkers should be cautious when testing a restore so that they do not inadvertently overwrite the current information on the device. Teleworkers should consult the documentation for the backup process to determine how the backups should be validated.

computer that is temporarily used for remote access. Some remote access methods perform basic information cleanup, such as clearing Web browser caches that might inadvertently hold sensitive information, but more extensive cleanup typically requires using a special utility, such as a disk scrubbing program specifically designed to remove all traces of information from a device. Many organizations offer their teleworkers assistance in removing information from personally owned devices. Another example of information destruction is shredding telework papers containing sensitive information once the papers are no longer needed.

■ **Erasing information from missing cell phones and PDAs.** If a cell phone or PDA is lost or stolen, occasionally its contents can be erased remotely. This prevents an attacker from obtaining any information from the device. The availability of this service depends on the capabilities of the product and the company providing network services for the product.

Each situation may require a different combination of protection options: for example, an organization might require one combination for IPsec VPN access from teleworker-owned computers and another combination for access to an individual application from third party-secured devices. Teleworkers should follow their organizations' requirements and recommendations for protecting sensitive information accessed with telework devices. Some organizations use the same requirements and recommendations for all types of information because of the difficulties in differentiating sensitive and nonsensitive information.

Teleworkers also need to ensure that they adequately protect their remote access-specific authenticators, such as passwords, personal identification numbers (PIN), and hardware tokens. Such authenticators should not be stored with the telework computer, nor should multiple authenticators be stored with each other (e.g., a password or PIN should not be written on the back of a hardware token).

Teleworkers should also be aware of how to handle threats involving *social engineering*, which is a general term for attackers trying to trick people into revealing sensitive information or performing certain actions, such as downloading and executing files that appear to be benign but are actually malicious. For example, an attacker might approach a teleworker in a coffee shop and ask to use the computer for a minute or offer to help the teleworker with using the computer. Teleworkers should be wary of any requests they receive that could lead to a security breach or the theft of a telework device.

If a teleworker suspects that a security breach (including loss or theft of materials) has occurred involving a telework device, remote access communications, removable media, or other telework components, the teleworker should immediately follow the organization's policy and procedures for reporting the possible breach. This is particularly important if any of the affected telework components contain sensitive information such as PII, so that the potential impact of a security breach is minimized.

4. Securing Home Networks and Using External Networks

An important part of telework and remote access security is applying security measures to the home networks to which the telework device normally connects.[6] A major component of home network security is securing other PCs and consumer devices on the home network. If any of these devices become infected with malware or are otherwise compromised, they could be used to attack the telework device or eavesdrop on its communications. Consequently, teleworkers should ensure that all devices on their home networks are secured properly. Teleworkers should also be cautious about allowing others to place devices on the teleworkers' wired and wireless home networks, in case one of these devices has been or will be compromised.

Sections 4.1 and 4.2 present recommendations for securing wired and wireless home networks, respectively. Section 4.3 briefly discusses the security implications of performing telework from external networks. Many of the recommendations made in Sections 4.1 through 4.3 may be challenging for many users to implement. Users who are unsure of how to implement these recommendations should seek expert assistance.

4.1 Wired Home Networks

Teleworkers should secure their wired home networks to help protect their telework devices. The most important part of securing most wired home networks is separating the home network from the network's ISP as much as possible. If a telework device connects directly to the teleworker's ISP, such as plugging the device directly into a cable modem, then the device becomes directly accessible from the Internet and is at very high risk of being attacked. To prevent this from occurring, the home network should have a security device between the ISP and the telework device. This is most commonly accomplished by using a broadband router (e.g., cable modem router, DSL router) or a firewall appliance.[7]

This security device should be configured to prevent computers outside the home network from initiating communications with any of the devices on the home network, including the telework device.[8] Even if each device uses a personal firewall, a firewall appliance or broadband router should also be used to provide an additional layer of security. For example, if a personal firewall on a computer malfunctioned, the appliance or router would still protect the computer from unsolicited network communications from external computers. In some cases, the appliance or router also can protect devices on the home network from each other—if the devices are logically separated by the appliance or router. For example, a router that has both wired and wireless interfaces might be able to prevent the spread of certain types of malware from a device on the wireless network to a device on the wired network, depending on the router's capabilities and configuration. However, such home network configurations are relatively complex to set up and maintain, so only users who are proficient in networking and security should consider implementing these configurations.

---

[6] Some telework devices, such as cell phones and laptops with wireless broadband network cards, do not use home networks.

[7] A firewall appliance should not be confused with a personal firewall, which is software based; a firewall appliance is a separate physical device. A firewall appliance for a home network cannot perform the rigorous firewalling (e.g., stateful inspection) that enterprise-class firewalls can provide. Firewall appliances are intended to provide an additional layer of security by reducing the number of attacks that reach the PCs on the home network.

[8] Some firewalls provide this protection through a feature known as network address translation (NAT). NAT translates the home network's external, public Internet Protocol (IP) address assigned by the ISP into multiple internal private IP addresses. This not only helps to prevent external computers from initiating connections to the home network computers, but it also allows the home network to use a single public IP address, even though multiple devices may exist on the home network. This may offer a cost savings for consumers (many ISPs charge fees for multiple IP addresses). However, NAT may also interfere with the use of an organization's remote access solutions, particularly VPNs, as well as the use of the IPv6 protocol, so teleworkers should check with their organizations if they experience problems with the organizations' VPN or IPv6 services while using NAT.

When installing and configuring firewall appliances or broadband routers, teleworkers should perform the security precautions described in the manufacturer's documentation. The following are some examples of possible precautions:[9]

■ Changing default passwords on the device so that attackers cannot use them to gain access to the device (lists of default passwords are widely available on the Internet)

■ Configuring the device so that it cannot be administered from outside the home network, preventing external attackers from taking control of the device

■ Configuring the device to silently ignore unsolicited requests sent to it, which essentially hides the device from malicious parties. Teleworkers should check with their ISP before configuring a device this way, because it could inadvertently interfere with necessary communications with the ISP's infrastructure.

■ Checking for updates and applying them periodically, as explained in the manufacturer's documentation—either automatically (typically daily or weekly) or manually (to be performed by the teleworker at least monthly)

■ For broadband routers, turning off or disabling built-in wireless access points (AP) that are not used.

The proper precautionary measures for a firewall appliance or broadband router vary greatly from device to device, so some or all of these options may not be applicable to many devices.

4.2   Wireless Home Networks

Wireless networking transfers information through the air between a telework device and a wireless AP.[10] If improperly configured, a wireless home network will transmit sensitive information without adequate protection, exposing it to other wireless devices in close proximity. Accordingly, teleworkers should secure their wireless home networks so that their remote access communications are protected. Teleworkers should follow the security recommendations from the documentation for the home network's wireless AP. Assuming that the network is using Institute of Electrical and Electronics Engineers (IEEE) 802.11 protocols (e.g., 802.11a/b/g/n), the following are examples of common security recommendations:

■ **Use strong encryption to protect communications.** An industry group called the Wi-Fi Alliance has created a series of product security certifications called Wi-Fi Protected Access (WPA), which include the WPA and WPA2 certifications. These certifications define sets of security requirements for wireless networking devices. Devices with wireless network cards that support either WPA or WPA2 can use their security features, such as encrypting network communications with the Advanced Encryption Security (AES) algorithm.[11] Recommended choices, in order with the most preferred option first, are as follows:

1. WPA2 with AES

2. WPA with AES

3. WPA with Temporal Key Integrity Protocol (TKIP).

---

[9]   If the manufacturer's documentation does not explicitly recommend any security precautions, teleworkers should consider implementing the examples, assuming that the appliance or router supports the configuration options listed in the examples.

[10]   A device can also wirelessly network directly with another device through what is known as an ad hoc wireless network. However, known security risks exist with ad hoc networks; therefore, this guide does not recommend their use.

[11]   AES is a Federal Information Processing Standards (FIPS) approved encryption algorithm, which means that it has been reviewed and approved by the Federal government as being sufficiently strong to protect information on Federal systems.

Wired Equivalent Privacy (WEP) is an earlier form of protection for wireless communications that has serious flaws. Attackers can easily circumvent WEP and gain access to the information being sent over the wireless network. If WEP is the only protection option available for a home network, users should configure it to use 128-bit encryption (which will somewhat slow attacks), use the organization's secure remote access solution (e.g., VPN) to protect their remote access communications, and avoid sending any sensitive information unprotected.

- **Use a WPA2, WPA, or WEP key** (depending on the option selected above). This key is a series of characters (either a password composed of letters, digits, and punctuation, or a hexadecimal number) that is used to limit access to a wireless network. A wireless AP can be configured to require each device to provide the same key as the one stored in the AP. Devices that do not know the key cannot use the wireless network. The key should be long and complex, making it difficult for others to guess. This should help to prevent people near the AP from gaining unauthorized access to the network.

- **Permit access for only particular wireless network cards.** Some APs can be configured to allow only specific devices to use the wireless network. This is accomplished by identifying the media access control (MAC) address of each device's wireless network card and entering the MAC address into a list on the AP. Because a MAC address should be unique to a particular network interface, specifying its MAC address in the AP can be helpful in preventing some unauthorized parties from gaining wireless network access.[12] (Consult a device's documentation to learn how to determine its MAC address.)

- **Change the default service set identifier (SSID).** An SSID is a name assigned to a wireless AP. The SSID allows people and devices to distinguish one wireless network from another. Most APs have a default SSID—often the manufacturer or product's name. If this default SSID is not changed, and another nearby wireless network has the same default SSID, then the teleworker's device might accidentally attempt to join the wrong wireless network.[13] Changing the SSID to something unusual—not the default value or an obvious value, such as "SSID" or "wireless"—makes it much less likely that a device will choose the wrong network.

- **Disable SSID broadcasts from the wireless AP.** Many wireless APs broadcast the SSID, which essentially advertises the existence of the AP to any computers in the vicinity. Configuring an AP so that it does not broadcast its SSID makes it less likely that people will inadvertently attempt to join the wireless network, but does not stop an attacker from doing so.

- **Disable AP administration through wireless communications.** Flaws are frequently identified in the administration utilities for wireless APs. If an AP has such a flaw, attackers in the vicinity could reconfigure it to disable its security features or use it to acquire access to the teleworker's home network or the Internet. To prevent such incidents, teleworkers should configure APs so that they can only be administered locally—such as running a cable between a computer and the AP—and not administered wirelessly or otherwise remotely.

---

[12] A knowledgeable attacker can circumvent MAC address lists by configuring his or her computer to pretend to use an authorized MAC address. MAC address lists are mainly helpful at preventing use of the wireless network by people who have no malicious intent, such as someone accidentally connecting to the network or someone looking for a way to get Internet access. Using MAC address lists provides an additional layer of security that can deter attackers (e.g., cause them to look for easier targets) but not stop them.

[13] If the teleworker's access point and telework device are configured to use encryption, the telework device will fail to join the other wireless network because the two networks are using different encryption keys. This is another benefit of using encryption for wireless communications.

4.3   External Networks

Teleworkers should be aware that networks other than their home networks are unlikely to provide much protection for their telework devices and communications, such as a laptop using a wireless hotspot at a coffee shop. For example, external networks may not encrypt network communications, making them susceptible to eavesdropping, particularly for wireless networks. Telework devices on external networks are also often directly accessible from the Internet. Some networks provide partial protection, such as blocking specific types of communications usually associated with malicious activity and checking communications for the most common known threats, such as widespread worms or spam messages.

Because there is usually no easy way for teleworkers to determine what protection an external network might be providing for their devices, teleworkers should assume that third-party networks are not providing any protection. Telework devices on third-party networks are generally at higher risk of being compromised than those on home networks, and their communications are also at higher risk of being monitored. Before using a third-party network, teleworkers should ensure that their devices are fully updated (see Section 5.1). The updates should be retrieved over a trusted network, such as the user's home network. When teleworkers use a third-party network to access their organization's computing resources, they should use a VPN or other secure remote access solution provided by the organization, and they should activate the secure remote access solution (e.g., establishing a VPN session) immediately after connecting to the third-party network.

5.   Securing Telework PCs

Teleworkers who use their own desktop or laptop PCs for telework should implement the recommendations presented in this section. These recommendations should be helpful in securing a PC's OS and primary applications. Teleworkers who do not need to secure telework PCs may skip this section.

Some of the recommendations made in this section may be challenging for many users to implement. Users who are unsure of how to implement these recommendations should seek expert assistance.

5.1   Software Updates

Many threats take advantages of vulnerabilities in software on PCs. Software manufacturers release updates for their software to eliminate these vulnerabilities. Accordingly, teleworkers should ensure that updates are applied regularly to the major software on their telework PCs. In addition to the OS, updating should include the following types of software:

- Web browsers
- Email clients
- Instant messaging clients
- Antivirus software
- Antispyware software
- Personal firewalls.

Teleworkers should review manufacturer documentation for each software program their PC contains in these categories to determine each program's update capabilities. Most major software programs provide built-in mechanisms to update themselves automatically. Teleworkers should enable these features so that the programs check for updates at least weekly, preferably daily. For any programs that do not offer automatic updating, the teleworker should determine from the documentation other available options, such as running an update feature from the application's menus every week or visiting the manufacturer's Web site weekly for updates and downloading and installing any available updates.

For a PC with slow connectivity, such as dial-up access, teleworkers should be cautious when configuring automatic software update features. Because many updates are very large, downloading them could consume all the network bandwidth on a slow link for hours at a time. This could make it difficult for teleworkers to send and receive email, access Web sites, and use the network in other ways while the download is occurring. Teleworkers could instead configure the software to download the updates at a time when no one needs to use the PC. Updates should still be performed at least weekly, preferably daily.

Some software manufacturers offer updates at no charge, whereas others require an annual fee or other payment to receive updates, such as paying a subscription fee to get the latest antivirus signatures. Most software manufacturers that charge a fee allow users to pay it through the manufacturer's Web site and receive updates within minutes of making payment.

5.2 User Accounts and Sessions

A PC can be configured with user accounts and passwords to restrict who can use the PC. This section explains how teleworkers can configure their telework PCs to prevent unauthorized access to their applications and data.

5.2.1 Use Accounts with Limited Privileges

On most OSs, user accounts can have full privileges or limited privileges. Accounts with full privileges, also known as *administrative accounts*, should be used only when performing PC management tasks, such as installing updates and application software, managing user accounts, and modifying OS and application settings. If a PC is attacked while an administrative account is in use, the attack will be able to inflict more damage to the PC. Therefore, user accounts should be set up to have limited privileges; such accounts are known as *daily use*, *limited*, or *standard user accounts*. Teleworkers should not use administrative accounts for general tasks, such as reading email and surfing the Web, because such tasks are common ways of infecting PCs with malware.

The primary disadvantages of having separate administrative and standard user accounts are that standard users might not be able to run some applications, especially ones designed for older OSs, or to install applications and OS or application updates. This could cause a significant delay in downloading and installing updates, as well as making other tasks less convenient for users. Some OSs have a feature that allows a person logged in as a standard user to perform individual administrative tasks by selecting a particular option.

Each person who uses the telework PC should have a separate standard user account. On most OSs, this keeps each person's data and settings (e.g., files, stored emails, Web browser bookmarks and security settings) private from other people using the PC. It also helps limit how much damage certain attacks can cause, such as damaging only one user's files, not all users' files.

5.2.2 Protect Accounts with Passwords

Each PC user account should have a password to prevent unauthorized people from using the PC—not only people with physical access to the PC, but also attackers attempting to contact the PC from other computers. Users should select strong passwords that cannot be guessed by attackers. The following are recommended practices for password selection:[14]

- **Select a sufficiently long password.** Longer passwords are more difficult to guess than shorter passwords of similar complexity (see below). The downside is that longer passwords are often more difficult for users to remember. Users should select passwords that are at least eight characters long. Passphrases, which are long passwords usually composed of multiple words, may be easier to remember than conventional passwords.

- **Create a complex password.** A variety of characters should be part of the password. For example, a password made of all lower case letters is a relatively simple password, but another password of the same length made of upper and lower case letters, digits, and symbols (such as punctuation marks) is relatively complex. The more complex the password is, the more difficult it will be for others to guess. Users should select passwords containing digits and/or symbols in addition to letters. Users should not create new passwords that are very similar to old passwords. For example, if the old password was "dahlia*1", the new password should not be "dahlia*2".

---

[14] Organizations may have additional requirements for the selection and management of passwords on personal PCs used for telework. Teleworkers should ensure that they meet any such requirements, in addition to the recommendations listed here.

- **Do not use password hints.** Password hints can be very helpful to people in guessing others' passwords and using them to gain unauthorized access to a PC. Users should not use password hints unless their PCs do not need protection from people with physical access to them.

- **Do not use the same password for other accounts.** Teleworkers should not use the same password for multiple accounts, such as organization and personal email accounts, instant messaging accounts, and e-commerce Web site accounts. If the password used for the telework PC is also used for other user accounts and an attacker learned one of the passwords, the attacker could then access the other accounts.

Teleworkers should change their passwords regularly, based on the interval specified in their organizations' password policies. This is necessary because if a password is unknowingly revealed to an unauthorized person or uncovered by malware or other automated attacks, the password could be used without authorization until the teleworker changes the password.

If an OS password is forgotten, especially for an administrative account, it may be difficult to regain access to the PC. Therefore, users should consider writing down their OS passwords and storing them in a physically secure location, such as a locked fire safe. Users should also safeguard their other passwords, such as application and Web site passwords. For example, some organizations provide cryptographic tokens to teleworkers that can be used to hold passwords. When the teleworker needs to retrieve a password, he or she authenticates to the token (such as entering a PIN into the token), and the token provides the password. The token helps prevent users from losing their passwords while also protecting the passwords from attackers. Another option for protecting application and Web site passwords is a password management utility, which is a program that can be used to generate, store, and access passwords securely. A teleworker typically enters a single password to gain access to all the passwords stored by the utility.

5.2.3 Protect User Sessions from Unauthorized Physical Access

It is important that user sessions be protected against unauthorized physical access. For example, if a PC is sitting unattended in an area that other people can access, anyone could walk up to the PC and masquerade as the user, such as sending email from the user's account, accessing the organization's remote access resources, making purchases from Web sites, or accessing sensitive information stored on the PC. To prevent such events, most OSs allow the user to lock the current session through menu options or a combination of keystrokes. Also, many OSs offer screensavers that activate automatically after the PC has been idle for a certain number of minutes, and can also be activated manually by the user on demand. Some of these screensavers can be configured to lock the PC and require the user to enter his or her password to unlock it. If a PC will be left unattended in an accessible area at any time, users should use a password-protected screensaver or manually lock their user sessions. However, users should be aware that these security features provide only short-term protection; someone who has access to the PC for an extended period of time can bypass these features and gain access to the user's session and data.

5.3 Networking Configuration

Most PCs can be configured to limit network access, which reduces the number of ways in which attackers can try to gain access to the PC. This section makes recommendations for configuring networking features to better protect the PC.

5.3.1 Disable Unneeded Networking Features

By default, most PCs provide several networking features that can provide communications and data sharing between PCs. Most teleworkers need to use only a few of these features. Because many attacks are network based, PCs should use only the necessary networking features. For example, file and printer sharing services, which allow other computers to access a telework PC's files and printers, should be disabled unless the PC shares its files or printers with other computers, or if a particular application on the PC requires the service to be enabled.[15] Other examples of services that might not be needed are IPv6 protocols,[16] wireless networking protocols (e.g., Bluetooth, IEEE 802.11a/b/g/n) and infrared ports. (Consult the PC's hardware and OS documentation for guidance on which network features should be disabled; if still unsure, seek expert assistance.)

5.3.2   Limit the Use of Remote Access Utilities

Some OSs offer features that allow a teleworker to get remote technical support assistance from a coworker, friend, product manufacturer, or others when running into problems with a PC. Many applications are also available that permit remote access to the PC from other computers. Although these features are convenient, they also increase the risk that the PC will be accessed by attackers. Therefore, such utilities should be kept disabled at all times except specifically when needed. The utilities should also be configured to require the remote person to be authenticated, usually with a username and password, before gaining access to the PC. (See the recommendations in Section 5.2.2 for choosing strong passwords.) Provide the username and password to the remote person in person, by phone, or by other means that cannot be monitored by attackers; do not send passwords through email messages, instant messaging, or other methods that do not provide protection for communications.

5.3.3   Configure Wireless Networking

An improperly configured wireless network could transmit sensitive information without protecting it properly, allowing people nearby to eavesdrop. Section 4.2 explains how to secure a wireless home network. In addition, PCs should be configured so that they do not automatically attempt to join wireless networks they detect. For example, a PC could join a neighbor's wireless home network instead of the teleworker's network; if that neighbor's network is improperly secured, then the teleworker's communications and computer could be at higher risk. Therefore, teleworkers should configure their PCs so they do not join detected wireless networks automatically. Teleworkers should also configure their PCs so that they cannot use ad hoc networking, which is a relatively easy way to attack a PC.

5.4   Attack Prevention

As explained in Section 2, no 100-percent solution exists for computer security; it is simply not possible to thwart every single attack. PCs should use a combination of software and software features that will stop most attacks, particularly malware. The types of software described in this section are antivirus and antispyware software, personal firewalls, spam and Web content filtering, and popup blocking. Changing a few settings on common applications, such as email clients and Web browsers, can also stop some attacks.

Although security tools can stop many attacks, teleworkers also need to practice safe computing habits. One of the most common ways that PCs are attacked is by users opening and executing files from unknown and untrusted sources. Teleworkers may download these files from Web sites, file sharing services, peer-to-peer programs, or other means, or they may be sent to teleworkers through email, instant messaging, and other communications services. These files often contain malware, and teleworkers

---

[15] It is particularly important to disable such services if the PC will be used on unsecured wireless networks, such as most wireless hotspots.

[16] IPv6 support is built in to newer OSs. Directions on disabling and enabling IPv6 support are available from OS vendors. Examples are Microsoft Vista (http://www.microsoft.com/technet/network/ipv6/ipv6faq.mspx) and Apple Mac OS X 10.4 (Chapter 5 of http://images.apple.com/server/pdfs/Tiger_Security_Config.pdf).

unknowingly infect their PCs by trying to use these files. Teleworkers should avoid using any files that are coming from unknown and untrusted sources. Other people using a teleworker's PC should also be made aware of safe computing habits.

5.4.1 Install and Configure Antivirus and Antispyware Software

The most effective tool for protecting PCs against malware is antivirus software, which is specifically designed to detect many forms of malware and prevent them from infecting PCs, as well as cleaning PCs that have already been infected. Because malware is the most common threat against PCs, NIST recommends that PCs use antivirus software at all times.[17] The antivirus software should be kept up-to-date, as described in Section 5.1.

Many brands of antivirus software are available, most of which offer similar functionality. NIST recommends configuring antivirus software to use the following types of functions:

- Automatically checking for and acquiring updates of signature or data definition files at least daily

- Scanning critical OS components, such as startup files, system basic input/output system (BIOS), and boot records

- Monitoring the behavior of common applications, such as email clients, Web browsers, file transfer and file sharing programs, and instant messaging software

- Performing real-time scans of each file as it is downloaded, opened, or executed

- Scanning all hard drives regularly to identify any file system infections, and optionally scanning removable media as well

- Handling files that are infected by attempting to *disinfect* them, which refers to removing malware from within a file, and *quarantining* them, which means that files containing malware are stored in isolation for future disinfection or examination

- Logging all significant events, such as the results of scans, the startup and shutdown of antivirus software, the installation of updates, and the discovery and handling of any instances of malware.

Most antivirus products can identify several types of malware, including viruses, worms, Trojan horses, and malicious mobile code.[18] Antivirus products offer varying levels of support for detecting spyware.[19] Separate antispyware utilities should be used to supplement any antivirus products that do not have robust spyware handling capabilities. Unlike antivirus software, which attempts to identify many types of malware, antispyware utilities specialize in malware and non-malware forms of spyware. Although some

---

[17] For some OSs, such as most Unix-based OSs, alternate types of anti-malware software, such as rootkit detectors, may be more effective than antivirus software at protecting the PCs from malware and should be used instead of antivirus software. Readers with such OSs should adjust the recommendations presented in this publication so that they apply to the types of anti-malware software most useful for their particular OSs.

[18] A *virus* is a program that self-replicates—makes copies of itself—by infecting files and distributing copies of itself to other files, programs, or computers. A *worm* is a self-replicating program that is completely self-contained and self-propagating. A *Trojan horse* is a program that appears to be benign but actually has a hidden malicious purpose. *Malicious mobile code* is software that is transmitted from a remote computer to be run on the local computer for malicious purposes, typically without the user's explicit instruction or knowledge. For more information on types of malware, see NIST Special Publication 800-83, *Guide to Malware Incident Prevention and Handling*, which is available at http://csrc.nist.gov/publications/PubsSPs html.

[19] There are many commercial and free programs that can detect many types of malware. There are also free programs that are more specialized. For example, antivirus software manufacturers sometimes release free utilities that find and remove a particular worm that has spread throughout the Internet.

antispyware utilities specialize in a particular form of spyware, such as browser plug-ins, most can detect many types of spyware and offer similar features to antivirus software. The updating and configuration recommendations made earlier in this section for antivirus software also apply to antispyware utilities.

5.4.2 Use Personal Firewalls

A *personal firewall* is a software program that monitors communications between a PC and other computers and that blocks communications that are unwanted. When properly configured, a personal firewall limits the ability of other computers to initiate communications with the telework PC. This can significantly reduce the exposure of the PC to network-based attacks, such as worms. A personal firewall can also be used to protect shared resources on a PC, such as file and print shares. Accordingly, a personal firewall should be installed and enabled on every telework PC. Personal firewalls should be configured to log significant events, such as blocked and allowed activity, the startup and shutdown of the firewall software, and firewall configuration changes, to assist in troubleshooting problems. All personal firewalls can monitor incoming communications, and some can also monitor outbound communications; the latter offers better security, but it can also inadvertently cause problems in using certain applications.

Although personal firewalls are important security controls for PCs, they can be relatively difficult to configure correctly. If a personal firewall is configured to be too restrictive, it could prevent some applications or OS functions from working correctly. For example, a personal firewall might prevent the use of file and print services. On the other hand, if a personal firewall is configured to be too permissive, it could permit attacks to compromise the PC. Teleworkers should read their personal firewall documentation carefully to gain a solid understanding of how it should be configured. If it is not clear, teleworkers should seek expert guidance on configuring their personal firewalls.[20]

Ideally, personal firewalls should deny all types of communications that teleworkers have not specifically approved as being permitted. This is known as a *deny by default* configuration because all communications that are not on the exception list are denied (blocked) automatically. Most firewalls can be configured to allow communications based on lists of authorized applications, such as Web browsers contacting Web servers and email clients sending and receiving email messages. Communications involving any other application are either denied automatically, or permitted or denied based on the teleworker responding to a prompt asking for a decision regarding the activity. For example, if a teleworker installs a new application and runs it for the first time, the firewall might ask the teleworker if that application should be allowed to access the Internet.

Unfortunately, this feature can be problematic. Personal firewalls often do not provide clear information on which application is attempting to use the network, so teleworkers struggle to determine if the activity is benign or malicious. If the nature of the activity is unclear, cautious teleworkers often choose to block the activity, but this may inadvertently disrupt legitimate activity. To avoid this problem, many teleworkers choose to permit access whenever asked, but this could support malicious activity. When unsure what to do, teleworkers should search for additional information about the service or software in question or ask someone with more security expertise for assistance.

Each PC should only have a single personal firewall enabled.[21] If multiple firewalls are enabled, they may interfere with each other. For example, one firewall might allow activity that the other one has been

---

[20] Configuring a personal firewall is often a complex task. Some firewalls have rules for specific protocols, services, or port numbers (e.g., File Transfer Protocol [FTP], Hypertext Transfer Protocol [HTTP], Simple Mail Transfer Protocol [SMTP]). For these firewalls, proper configuration may require networking and security experience.

[21] Having multiple personal firewalls installed on a single PC is fine as long as only one is enabled at a time. For example, some OSs have built-in personal firewalls, but a user might install a third-party firewall onto the computer because the third-party firewall is part of a security software suite that includes antivirus software and other security applications.

configured to block. This could slow the performance of the PC, cause applications to stop functioning properly, and weaken the computer's security. When enabling a firewall, teleworkers should verify that the firewall's functionality is enabled for every network interface on the PC, including wired and wireless network cards, dial-up modems, and VPNs.

Many personal firewalls offer additional security features. For example, some firewalls can stop all network access to and from the PC when it is idle, such as after 15 minutes of inactivity. When the teleworker returns to the computer, network access is restored. Although this helps to protect the PC, it can also prevent the PC from downloading updates and disrupt user services such as instant messaging. Another feature that some firewalls offer is the ability to require teleworkers to enter a password before accessing the firewall's configuration settings. This protects the configuration from being inadvertently or purposely altered by a user.

Teleworkers should be aware that most firewalls are frequently stopping unwanted activity. For example, attackers are constantly performing automated scans for targets, and worms and other malware are constantly trying to infect more PCs. Teleworkers should not be alarmed by notices from their firewall that indicate that incoming connections were blocked or that a specific attack was attempted. If a firewall indicates that the PC was just scanned for a particular worm, this does not in any way indicate that the PC has actually been infected with a worm. Attackers often scan thousands of hosts per minute, essentially at random.

5.4.3   Enable and Configure Content Filtering Software

Content filtering is the process of monitoring communications such as email and Web pages, analyzing them for suspicious content, and preventing the delivery of suspicious content to users. Two common types of content filtering are spam filtering software and Web content filtering software.

Spam—unsolicited email—is often used to deliver spyware and other forms of malware to users. Spam is also frequently used for performing phishing attacks, which are deceptive computer-based means to trick individuals into disclosing sensitive personal information. Spam filtering software analyzes emails to search for spam characteristics, and typically places messages that appear to be spam in a separate email folder. Most organizations perform spam filtering for their users; however, because spam filtering is subjective, some spam will still reach users, and some desired email messages will accidentally be classified as spam. Still, spam filtering software can significantly reduce the amount of spam that reaches users. Many email clients also offer some helpful spam filtering capabilities.

Users can refine spam-filtering capabilities through the following customization options:

■ **Blacklists.** A *blacklist* is a list of email senders who have previously sent spam to a user. When a user receives a spam message, he or she can request that the sender's email address be added to a blacklist. This will cause future emails from the same sender to be classified as spam automatically.

■ **Whitelists.** A *whitelist* is a list of email senders that are known to be benign, such as coworkers, friends, and family. A user can add their email addresses to a whitelist, which will cause their future emails to not be classified as spam. Spam filtering accidentally classifies some emails as spam that are not, but a whitelist overrides that classification and ensures that emails from trusted senders are received by the user.

■ **Bayesian Spam Filters.** A *Bayesian spam filter* determines the likelihood that a particular email message is spam, based on a comparison of the email's characteristics with those of previously received spam messages. When a user receives email, the user corrects any errors that the spam filtering software has made. The Bayesian filter then analyzes the benign messages and the spam to record their characteristics. For example, a Bayesian filter might record that a user has received 35 spam messages containing the phrase "FREE FREE FREE" but no benign messages with that phrase. When a user receives a new email, the filter looks for that phrase, as well as any other characteristics associated with benign or spam messages, and assigns a spam probability to the message. The effectiveness of Bayesian filters depends on users reviewing all their emails and ensuring each is marked correctly as being spam or not.

Web content filtering software typically works by comparing a Web site address that a user attempts to access with a list of known bad Web sites. Although the primary purpose of Web content filtering software is to prevent access to inappropriate materials, many also contain lists of Web sites that are known as hostile, such as those attempting to distribute malware to visitors or hosting phishing Web sites. Web content filtering software might inadvertently classify benign content as inappropriate or vice versa.

From a telework PC security perspective, spam content filtering technologies are strongly recommended for all email use; Web content filtering technologies also can be helpful but are considered optional.[22] All content filtering products that are used should be kept up-to-date to ensure that their detection is as accurate as possible.

5.5 Primary Application Configuration

Many attacks, particularly malware, take advantage of features provided by common applications such as email clients, Web browsers, instant messaging clients, and office productivity suites. By default, applications often are configured to favor functionality over security. Accordingly, teleworkers should consider disabling unneeded features and capabilities from applications, particularly those that are commonly exploited by malware. Teleworkers should also consider configuring applications to filter content and stop other activity that is likely to be malicious. Examples of application settings to consider are listed below. Teleworkers should be aware that a single PC might have multiple Web browsers, email clients, instant messaging clients, and office productivity suites installed, each of which may have different features and configuration settings.[23]

Teleworkers should also consider their organization's policies regarding application use. For example, many organizations forbid the use of peer-to-peer software, file sharing programs, and VoIP software on organization computers because of the increased security risks associated with the software. Teleworkers should remove software that is forbidden by policy from their telework computers to better protect the organization's information. In general, teleworkers should install and use only known and trusted software on their telework PCs.

5.5.1 Web Browsers

Teleworkers should consider adopting the following recommendations for the Web browsers on their telework PCs:

- **Use a different brand of Web browser for telework.** Multiple brands of Web browsers (e.g., Microsoft Internet Explorer, Mozilla Firefox, Apple Safari, Opera) can be installed on a single PC. Accessing Web sites containing malicious content is one of the most common ways for PCs to be

---

[22] These recommendations are for telework PCs, and assume that the organization is also performing spam and Web content filtering on the teleworker's remote access communications. If the organization is not providing these services, then teleworkers should use both spam and Web content filtering on their telework PCs.

[23] Many manufacturers document their security recommendations in their product documentation or on their Web sites. Some manufacturers also make security checklists available for securing their operating systems, applications, and devices. Many of these checklists are posted on the NIST Security Checklists for IT Products site, located at http://csrc.nist.gov/checklists/.

attacked, such as spyware plug-ins being installed in a browser. To reduce the likelihood that such attacks could impact telework, teleworkers can use one brand of browser for telework only and another brand of browser for all other Web site access. This separates the telework-related data within one browser from the data within the other browser, providing better protection for the telework data (although this alone cannot adequately secure browser data). Having a separate brand of browser for telework also allows the teleworker to secure it more tightly, such as disabling all forms of mobile code (e.g., Java, ActiveX) that are not required for telework (see Section 5.5.2 for more information on mobile code).

- **Restrict Web browser cookies.** A *cookie* is a small file that stores information for a Web site. Many Web sites place cookies on users' computers. A *persistent cookie* stays on a computer to allow a Web site to identify the Web site's user. Unfortunately, if someone else uses the same user account on the computer, some Web sites that use cookies may think that the two people are really the same person. The Web sites might then allow the second person to gain access to the first person's information on the Web sites. Persistent cookies may also store sensitive information, such as passwords or account numbers, that could be accessed by other people using the same computer. Another type of cookie, a *session cookie*, is valid only for a single Web site session. Session cookies do not usually contain personal information. Most Web browsers can be configured to permit all session cookies and to permit persistent cookies to be set only for the same Web site that the user visited (*first-party cookies*), not for the Web sites of advertisers and others (*third-party cookies*). This balances the preservation of users' privacy with the functionality that cookies can provide for Web site usage.

- **Block popup windows.** Nearly all Web browsers support the use of *popup windows*, which are standalone Web browser panes that open automatically when a Web page is loaded or a user performs an action designed to trigger a popup window. Many popup windows contain advertising, but they are increasingly being used as a way to attack computers. Some popup windows are crafted to resemble legitimate system message boxes or Web sites and can trick users into going to phony Web sites, including sites used for phishing, or authorizing changes to their computers, among other malicious actions. For example, a popup window may tell a user that the computer is infected with spyware and to click on OK to disinfect it. By clicking on OK, the user unwittingly permits spyware or other types of malware to be installed on the computer. To control popup windows, teleworkers should either configure their Web browsers to block them or use third-party popup blocking utilities that can block them. Both options prevent popup windows from opening and indicate to the teleworker that a popup window was blocked. If the teleworker did not want the window to be blocked, he or she could then choose to permit that particular popup window or all popup windows from a trusted Web site, such as the organization's remote access Web site.

- **Enable phishing filter capabilities.** Some browsers can detect possible phishing attempts and warn the user before allowing the user to visit a suspected phishing site. Teleworkers should check their browser's documentation to see if it offers a phishing filter, and if so, enable it.

- **Remove unneeded browser plug-ins.** A *plug-in* is a utility that works in conjunction with a Web browser to enhance the browser's capabilities. Most plug-ins are beneficial, but some plug-ins are malicious. Teleworkers should periodically review the plug-ins installed in their browsers and uninstall all plug-ins that are unneeded or unknown to the teleworkers. If a necessary plug-in is accidentally uninstalled, the teleworker is usually prompted to download and install it the next time the teleworker accesses content that requires the plug-in.

- **Protect sensitive information stored by the browser.** Browsers may store sensitive information on behalf of users, such as cached Web site passwords, digital certificates, and encryption keys. Some browsers have options for strongly protecting this information. Typically, the browser requires a user to enter a master password, which is used solely to protect the sensitive information. Teleworkers should check their browser's documentation to determine if it offers a protection option, and if so, enable it and set a master password.

- **Prevent Web site passwords from being recalled automatically.** Most browsers can save passwords that have been entered into Web sites. However, many browsers also offer auto-fill or auto-complete options that recall stored passwords and enter them into password text boxes automatically. This could allow someone else who accesses a telework device to gain access to various Web sites posing as the teleworker. To prevent this, teleworkers should configure their Web browsers so that they do not use auto-fill or auto-complete functions for usernames and passwords.

- **Run Web browsers with the least privileges possible.** Some Web browsers, such as Microsoft Internet Explorer 7 running on Windows Vista, can run in a mode that offers low privileges, which means that actions performed within the Web browser can affect the computer in very limited ways. This helps prevent some attacks sent through Web browsers from succeeding and limits the damage caused by attacks that do succeed. Teleworkers should run their Web browsers with the least privileges possible.

5.5.2 Email Clients

Teleworkers should consider adopting the following recommendations for each email client on their telework PCs:

- **Prevent automatic loading of remote email images.** Most email clients can be configured not to automatically load remote graphics pointed to by emails. This is particularly helpful for thwarting a form of spyware known as a Web bug. With this configuration setting, the outline of an unloaded Web bug appears as a small box within the email, and the teleworker's activity cannot be tracked unless the teleworker chooses to have the image loaded.

- **Limit mobile code execution.** Mobile code is a way for a remote computer, such as a Web site, to run programs on a teleworker's device. Email messages can carry malicious mobile code that attempts to infect the device from which the messages are read. To prevent infections, most email clients can be configured to permit only the required forms of mobile code (e.g., JavaScript, ActiveX, Java). Teleworkers should consider disabling mobile code support in their email clients, with the understanding that the full content of certain benign email messages might not be available.

- **Set default message reading format and sending format to plain text.** Many email clients allow users to specify the default format for reading and sending emails. The most commonly used formats are plain text and Hypertext Markup Language (HTML). Because malware, phishing, and other types of attacks often take advantage of features offered by HTML, it is preferable that the default message format be set to plain text. This will result in emails being displayed as text only, which means that pictures, hyperlinks, and other content provided through HTML would be omitted or displayed only through alternative text. Also, sending emails as plain text is helpful to other security-conscious users who prefer to read email messages in plain text. Another advantage of plain text emails is that they can be displayed properly on all types of devices, including cell phones and PDAs.

- **Disable automatic previewing and opening of email messages.** Some email-based malware may be activated and infect a computer when the malicious email is previewed or opened. Many email clients can be configured to preview or open email messages automatically. This can provide an easy way for malware to infect a computer. Accordingly, email clients should be configured not to preview or open email messages automatically. This gives teleworkers an opportunity to identify and delete an email that appears to be suspicious, based on the sender, recipient, subject, and other identifying information that can be reviewed without viewing the entire email.

■ **Enable spam filtering.** Section 5.4.3 has additional information concerning this issue.

5.5.3 Instant Messaging Clients

Teleworkers should consider adopting the following recommendations for each instant messaging client on their telework PCs:

■ **Suppress the display of email addresses.** If the teleworker's displayed name or supporting information includes an email address, this may be harvested by malware or malicious users, then used in future attacks.

■ **Restrict file transfers.** If the software can transfer files with other instant messaging users, it should be configured to prompt the teleworker before permitting a file transfer to begin. File transfers are a common way to transfer malware to other computers and infect them.

5.5.4 Office Productivity Suites

Teleworkers should consider adopting the following recommendations for each office productivity suite on their telework PCs:

■ **Restrict macro use.** Applications such as word processors and spreadsheets often contain macro languages that certain types of viruses use. Most common applications with macro capabilities offer security features that permit macros only from trusted locations or prompt the user to approve or reject each attempt to run a macro. The prompting feature can be effective at stopping macro-based malware threats.

■ **Limit personal information.** Many office productivity tools allow personal information, such as name, initials, mailing address, and phone number, to be stored with each document created. Although the most basic information (typically, name and initials) are often needed for collaboration features and edit tracking, information such as mailing addresses and phone numbers is not. Personal information becomes embedded within document files and may inadvertently be distributed with files to others. Teleworkers should not enter any more personal information than necessary into the user settings of office productivity tools. For some word processors, teleworkers can use sanitization utilities that remove personal information from documents, as well as comments, tracked changes, and other information that might be embedded in documents but should not be part of the final document.

■ **Use secured folders for application files.** Most office productivity applications allow users to define default locations for saving documents and holding temporary files, including auto-save and backup copies of documents. This can be very helpful at protecting application files from unauthorized access by others. Teleworkers should also store their custom dictionary entries in a user-specific file stored in one of their protected folders.

5.6 Remote Access Software Configuration

As described in Section 2, teleworkers may have to install remote access software onto their telework PCs or configure software built into the PC's OS. This software should be configured based on the organization's requirements and recommendations. In many cases, the remote access software will be preconfigured by the organization so that teleworkers do not have to be concerned about configuring it. In general, remote access software should be configured so that only the necessary functions are enabled. Teleworkers should also ensure that whenever updates to the remote access software are available, that they are acquired and installed. If the organization provides the updates, teleworkers should make sure that they will be notified when updates are available.

5.7   Security Maintenance and Monitoring

Teleworkers should maintain their telework PCs' security on an ongoing basis. Common responsibilities are as follows:

■   Confirming periodically that the OS and primary applications are up-to-date. Many software programs have a menu option or other mechanism that displays the update status, such as the number of updates that have not yet been applied or the most recent date the software was updated.

■   Checking the status of security software periodically to ensure that it is still enabled, configured properly, and up-to-date. Some operating systems offer security dashboards that show the current status of the security software. Checking the software's status should also include verifying that the regular scans performed by antivirus software and antispyware software have not found any infections on the PC. If an infection is still present, the teleworker should follow the security software's instructions for disinfecting the PC.

■   Creating a new user account whenever another person needs to start using the PC, as well as disabling or deleting a user account whenever the associated person no longer needs to use the PC. All the user accounts should be reviewed periodically to ensure that only the necessary accounts are enabled.

■   Changing the teleworker's PC password regularly in accordance with the organization's password policy.

■   Periodically identifying security issues on the PC. Some OSs offer utilities that can be run to check the PC for potential problems. These utilities can identify missing software updates and incorrect security settings and can provide recommendations for fixing problems. However, understanding the reports that these utilities produce and properly implementing recommended solutions can require someone with considerable security expertise. Teleworkers without sufficient expertise should seek expert assistance before implementing any unclear recommendations.

Teleworkers also need to investigate any cases in which the PC begins to display unusual behavior. Generally, the best first step is to ensure that the computer's software (especially antivirus and antispyware software) is fully up-to-date; then, the entire computer should be scanned using the antivirus and antispyware software. If any malware is detected, it should be removed using the antivirus and antispyware software; if no malware is detected, then the next step should be to reboot the computer, which clears many errors. If that is ineffective, then additional troubleshooting steps need to be performed. Examples are as follows:

■   Checking antivirus and antispyware manufacturer Web sites for instances of malware that cause the unusual behavior being seen

■   Uninstalling and reinstalling an application that is not functioning properly

■   Searching the OS manufacturer's Web site for information on similar problems

■   Using troubleshooting utilities that can provide insights into what is happening on the PC.

If the problem still cannot be resolved, or the teleworker does not have sufficient knowledge to perform these troubleshooting steps, the teleworker should seek expert assistance, such as contacting the organization's help desk if the organization provides support for personally owned telework computers. Teleworkers can assist with troubleshooting by collecting and documenting information regarding the problems. Some OSs provide features that automate this process, and some PC manufacturers install utilities on their PCs designed specifically for this purpose. Teleworkers should consult the PC's hardware and OS manuals for information regarding such features. Teleworkers also should preserve error messages by performing a screen capture, copying and pasting the error message into a file or email, or writing down the error message verbatim on paper. (The appropriate technique should be selected based on the complexity of the error message and the PC's support for performing screen captures, if any.)

6. Securing Telework Consumer Devices

Teleworkers who use their own consumer devices for telework, particularly cell phones, PDAs, and smart phones (hybrid cell phone/PDA devices, such as the BlackBerry and Windows Mobile), should implement the recommendations presented in this section. Teleworkers who do not need to secure consumer devices can skip this section.

A wide variety of consumer devices exist, and the security features available for these devices also vary widely. Some devices offer only a few basic features, whereas others offer sophisticated features similar to those offered by PCs. This does not necessarily imply that more security features are better; in fact, many devices offer more security features because the capabilities they provide, such as wireless networking and instant messaging, make them more susceptible to attack than devices without these capabilities. In general, consumer devices currently face fewer threats than PCs, but threats against consumer devices are increasing. The variety in security features makes it infeasible to create specific recommendations that apply to all consumer devices; therefore, teleworkers should consult the documentation provided by their device manufacturers and service providers (e.g., cellular service) and follow their security recommendations. General recommendations are as follows:

- **Limit access to the device.** Most consumer devices allow the owner to restrict access by setting a PIN or password; some also support more sophisticated authentication mechanisms, such as biometrics (e.g., the owner's thumbprint). Using some sort of authenticator prevents or deters access to the teleworker's information and service by a person who gains unauthorized physical access to the device. Some devices can also be configured to lock themselves automatically after an idle period; a person attempting to use the device when it is locked must authenticate again to unlock it.[24] PINs and passwords should be changed periodically and whenever teleworkers suspect that someone else may know them.

- **Disable necessary networking capabilities except when they are needed.** Many consumer devices offer multiple types of networking capabilities, such as IEEE 802.11a/b/g/n, Bluetooth, and infrared.[25] Attackers can try to use these capabilities to access information on the device or use the device's services. This can be prevented by disabling each networking capability that is not used, and by enabling necessary capabilities only when they are going to be used. For example, if a person only uses a Bluetooth earpiece occasionally with a cell phone, then the teleworker could enable the cell phone's Bluetooth capability only when the teleworker wants to use the earpiece and disable it when the teleworker is done with the earpiece. Each enabled networking capability increases the risk of successful attacks, so teleworkers should consider the relative risk of each form of networking before enabling it (for example, enabling Bluetooth or infrared in a crowded public area is generally riskier than enabling these capabilities in a private home).

- **Use additional security software, if appropriate.** Antivirus software and personal firewall software are available for some consumer devices, particularly those with traditional PDA capabilities, such as downloading email messages and synchronizing documents with PCs. If feasible, antivirus software should be installed and enabled on consumer devices and configured to monitor activity on each network interface. Personal firewall software should be installed and enabled on consumer devices that use Transmission Control Protocol/Internet Protocol (TCP/IP) networking and configured to restrict activity on each TCP/IP interface. Both antivirus software and personal firewall software

---

[24] Some devices can be configured to wipe themselves after a certain number of failed authentication attempts. If this feature is enabled, teleworkers should maintain current backups of the information on the device so that it can be restored if excessive authentication attempts cause the device to be wiped.

[25] In addition, some devices can accept third-party networking cards to provide additional networking capabilities. Consult the cards' documentation as well and remove or disable the cards if they are not needed.

should be kept up-to-date. Section 5.4 contains additional information on antivirus software and personal firewalls.[26]

■ **Keep devices updated.** Some consumer devices can be updated or patched to eliminate known security flaws. Devices that support updating may do so directly (e.g., the teleworker selects an option on the device to get an update) or indirectly (e.g., the teleworker downloads a patch onto a PC, and then installs the patch onto the consumer device through a data cable connecting the two). If a device does support updating, teleworkers should follow the provided instructions to ensure that security updates are identified, acquired, and installed regularly, at least monthly, preferably weekly. Some updates cause all data on the device to be lost, so teleworkers should check for that and perform a full device backup before applying such an update.

■ **Configure applications to support security.** Many applications on consumer devices, such as Web browsers, are often configured by default to favor functionality over security. Accordingly, teleworkers should consider disabling unneeded application features and configuring applications to stop or block activity that is likely to be malicious. Section 5.5 provides configuration recommendations for Web browsers, email clients, and instant messaging clients on personal computers; these recommendations should also be applied to consumer devices to the extent possible.

Teleworkers should be cautious about connecting consumer devices to other computers, such as synchronizing data between a PDA and a desktop computer. Malware could be transmitted from one device to another during a synchronization. Also, a synchronization could inadvertently cause sensitive information to be transferred from one device to another, and the second device might not be configured to provide adequate protection to that information, putting it at higher risk of exposure. Before connecting a consumer device to another computer, teleworkers should ensure that the consumer device and the computer to which it will be attached have both been properly secured.

Teleworkers should also be cautious about downloading and installing software onto a consumer device if the software is not being provided by either the organization or the device's manufacturer. An example is downloading games from an unfamiliar Web site. Such software could reduce the security of the device if the software is not configured properly, or the software itself could contain malware that would infect the device. The software could also inadvertently disrupt other applications, including security software.

---

[26] Some types of devices are less susceptible to particular categories of attacks than others. For some types of devices, malware and other automated attacks are not a significant threat, and antivirus software or personal firewalls may not even be available.

7. Considering the Security of Third-Party Devices

Teleworkers often want to perform remote access from devices owned by third parties, such as checking email from a kiosk computer at a conference. However, when a third party is responsible for securing a device, teleworkers typically do not know if it has been secured properly. Consequently, a teleworker could perform remote access from a compromised device—for example, one infected with malware intended to steal information from users, such as their passwords or email messages.

Many organizations either forbid third-party devices to be used for remote access or permit only limited use, such as for Web-based email. If an organization permits the use of third-party devices for telework, teleworkers should think about the environment of a third-party device before deciding whether or not to use it. There is generally more risk in using third-party devices than in using the teleworkers' own devices because of uncertainty as to how the third-party devices have been secured; however, some third-party devices are reasonably secured. Teleworkers should consider who is responsible for securing a third-party device and who can access the device. For example, a kiosk provided at a conference for attendees only is more likely to be reasonably secure than a kiosk in a hotel lobby available to the general public. Whenever possible, teleworkers should not use publicly accessible devices for telework, including remote access to email and other applications.

Teleworkers should avoid using any third-party devices for performing sensitive functions or accessing sensitive information, unless absolutely necessary. If a teleworker is not reasonably confident of the security of a third-party device, the teleworker should be cautious and avoid using it. Many teleworkers choose not to use any third party-secured devices for remote access because of security concerns.

In some cases, teleworkers have an alternative to using a third-party device. If a teleworker has their own telework device but does not have Internet access, the teleworker may be able to use the Internet access method provided to a third-party device. For example, a teleworker may be able to unplug the wired network connection from a kiosk computer and plug it into the teleworker's own device. Teleworkers should ensure that this use of the network connection is permissible before attempting to use it. Also, teleworkers should be aware that in some environments, plugging a network cable into the computer will not grant it Internet access for technical or administrative reasons.

Appendix A—Additional Security Considerations for Telework

In addition to securing telework devices and home networks, there are additional security-related considerations for telework. For example, teleworkers should consider the relative security of phone services, such as cordless phones, cellular phones, and Voice over Internet Protocol (VoIP) services. Other possible security concerns include the use of wireless personal area network (WPAN) technologies, such as Bluetooth and infrared; use of wireless broadband network technologies; and secure destruction of removable media, printed materials, and other forms of media that may contain sensitive information. This appendix provides recommendations for each topic.

A.1 Phone Services

Depending on the sensitivity of telework communications, telephone security may be a consideration. The various choices for telephones and telephone services span a wide spectrum of privacy capabilities. At the low end are older cordless phones, whose calls may be picked up by walkie-talkies, baby monitors, and radio scanners; at the high end are corded phones. The most commonly used options are summarized below.

- **Corded phones using traditional wired telephone networks.** Physical connections are required to intercept communications involving traditional corded telephones that use wired telephone networks, so they are sufficiently secure for typical telework. Security for corded phones used with VoIP networks is described below.

- **Cordless phones using traditional wired telephone networks.** Cordless phone communications can be intercepted by eavesdroppers within physical proximity of the phone, often a few hundred yards at most. Cordless phones used for telework should employ spread spectrum technology, which uses a rapidly changing set of frequencies to scramble transmissions, thus reducing the risk of eavesdropping. Security for cordless phones used with VoIP networks is described below.

- **Cellular phones.** Most cell phones use digital technology, and their transmissions are scrambled to deter eavesdropping. Digital cell phones should be acceptable for typical telework. Older cellular phones use analog technology. Analog calls can be intercepted by individuals with scanning equipment, so teleworkers should avoid using analog cell phones for discussions involving sensitive or proprietary information.

- **Voice over IP.** There are many services that offer local and long-distance phone service over the Internet. Known as VoIP, the services convert speech to Internet messages and transmit them to a facility that interfaces with the telephone network. The party on the other end can be using any type of phone service, not just VoIP. From a security standpoint, this type of connection may be susceptible to eavesdropping because it may be carried over the local network, the Internet service provider's network, and sometimes the Internet. Because of the potential for vulnerabilities in one or more of these networks, communications carried over VoIP should not be considered secure unless some form of encryption is used. Many VoIP services now provide strong encryption, so teleworkers interested in using VoIP for telework discussions involving sensitive or proprietary information should first check with the VoIP provider to see if communications are encrypted.

A.2 WPAN Technologies

WPANs are small-scale wireless networks that require no infrastructure to operate. A WPAN is typically used by a few devices in a single room to communicate without the need to physically connect devices with cables. Examples include using a wireless keyboard or mouse with a computer, printing wirelessly, synchronizing a personal digital assistant (PDA) with a computer, and allowing a wireless headset or earpiece to be used with a cell phone. The two most commonly used types of technologies for WPANs are Bluetooth and infrared. Although these two technologies have similar capabilities, they also have a few important differences. Infrared requires an unobstructed line of sight between the two devices using it, whereas Bluetooth does not. Furthermore, devices using infrared generally have to be within a meter (a few feet) of each other, whereas Bluetooth devices can be up to 100 meters (300 feet) apart, depending on output power.

As Sections 5 and 6 mention, teleworkers should disable Bluetooth and infrared when they are not in use. In addition, Bluetooth users should use a personal identification number (PIN) that is at least eight characters long, preferably one that includes letters and digits. This makes it more difficult for an attacker to guess the PIN and gain access to the Bluetooth devices. For Bluetooth devices that do not support the use of long PINs (some permit only four-digit PINs), teleworkers should choose hard-to-guess PINs. Teleworkers should also configure their Bluetooth devices to encrypt their communications, if the devices support it; the devices' documentation should provide the necessary information on configuring encryption capabilities.

A.3   Wireless Broadband Data Network Technologies

Cellular phone service providers offer wireless broadband data networks, a form of mobile networking for laptops and other types of computers. This technology allows a computer to have wireless access to the Internet from nearly any location. Because of the nature of cellular communications, it is much more difficult for an attacker to eavesdrop on wireless broadband networks than WLANs, but it is still possible. Therefore, teleworkers should assume that wireless broadband communications are not sufficiently secure for transmitting sensitive information. Teleworkers should consult with their organization to determine what protection the organization's remote access solution provides before using wireless broadband to send or receive sensitive information.

A.4   Information Destruction

When a teleworker-owned computer is no longer going to be used, it should be prepared for retirement. The computer's built-in storage devices, such as hard drives, often contain information that teleworkers might not want others to see, including their organizations' files and their personal information, such as files from tax return software. Even if the teleworker deletes all of the files from the computer, curious people who get access to the computer might be able to recover the files using free or inexpensive software utilities specifically designed to recover deleted files. Accordingly, teleworkers should ensure that all data on their computers' built-in storage devices is wiped out before donating, selling, or discarding a computer. Methods of performing these actions are as follows:

- **Use a third-party disk scrubbing utility.** Several commercial and open source software products are available that are specially designed to remove traces of data from computers. Follow the manufacturer directions for removing data from the hard drive.

- **Retain the hard drive.** Following the instructions in the computer manufacturer's documentation, a teleworker can remove the hard drive from the computer. If other people want to use the computer in the future, they can purchase a new hard drive and install an operating system (OS) onto the computer. This is the best option if the computer is no longer functioning properly, preventing the use of disk scrubbing utilities.

- **Destroy the hard drive.** Hard drives can be degaussed, which involves applying a magnetic field to the drive that makes it unusable. Hard drives can also be shredded or otherwise physically destroyed through specialized equipment and services.

Teleworkers also need to ensure that removable media, printed materials, and other forms of media that may contain sensitive information are also destroyed. Many organizations provide information destruction services for their teleworkers, such as scrubbing or destroying hard drives and shredding removable media and printed materials.

Appendix B—Glossary

Selected terms used in the publication are defined below.

Administrative Account: A user account with full privileges intended to be used only when performing personal computer (PC) management tasks, such as installing updates and application software, managing user accounts, and modifying operating system (OS) and application settings.

Blacklist: A list of email senders who have previously sent spam to a user.

Consumer Device: A small, usually mobile computer that does not run a standard PC OS. Examples of consumer devices are networking-capable personal digital assistants (PDA), cell phones, and video game systems.

Content Filtering: The process of monitoring communications such as email and Web pages, analyzing them for suspicious content, and preventing the delivery of suspicious content to users.

Cookie: A small file that stores information for a Web site on a user's computer.

Daily Use Account: See "Standard user account."

Disinfect: To remove malware from within a file.

Malicious Code: See "Malware."

Malware: A computer program that is covertly placed onto a computer with the intent to compromise the privacy, accuracy, or reliability of the computer's data, applications, or OS. Common types of malware threats include viruses, worms, malicious mobile code, Trojan horses, rootkits, and spyware.

Personal Computer (PC): A desktop or laptop computer running a standard PC OS (e.g., Windows Vista, Windows XP, Linux/UNIX, and Mac OS X).

Personal Firewall: A software program that monitors communications between a PC and other computers and blocks communications that are unwanted.

Phishing: Deceptive computer-based means to trick individuals into disclosing sensitive personal information.

Popup Window: A standalone Web browser pane that opens automatically when a Web page is loaded or a user performs an action designed to trigger a popup window.

Quarantine: To store files containing malware in isolation for future disinfection or examination.

Remote Access: The ability for an organization's users to access its non-public computing resources from locations other than the organization's facilities.

Remote System Control: Remotely using a computer at an organization from a telework computer.

Security Controls: See "Security Protections."

Security Protections: Measures against threats that are intended to compensate for a computer's security weaknesses.

Service Set Identifier (SSID): A name assigned to a wireless AP.

Social Engineering: A general term for attackers trying to trick people into revealing sensitive information or performing certain actions, such as downloading and executing files that appear to be benign but are actually malicious.

Spam: Unsolicited email.

Standard User Account: A user account with limited privileges that will be used for general tasks such as reading email and surfing the Web.

Telecommuting: See "Telework."

Telework: The ability for an organization's employees and contractors to conduct work from locations other than the organization's facilities.

Telework Device: A PC or consumer device used for performing telework.

Virtual Private Network (VPN): A tunnel that connects the teleworker's computer to the organization's network.

Vulnerability: A security weakness in a computer.

Whitelist: A list of email senders known to be benign, such as a user's coworkers, friends, and family.

Appendix C—Acronyms and Abbreviations

Acronyms and abbreviations used in this guide are defined below.

AES	Advanced Encryption Standard
AP	Access Point
BIOS	Basic Input/Output System
DSL	Digital Subscriber Line
FIPS	Federal Information Processing Standards
FISMA	Federal Information Security Management Act
FTP	File Transfer Protocol
HTML	Hypertext Markup Language
HTTP	Hypertext Transfer Protocol
IEEE	Institute of Electrical and Electronics Engineers, Inc.
IP	Internet Protocol
IPsec	Internet Protocol Security
ISP	Internet Service Provider
IT	Information Technology
ITL	Information Technology Laboratory
MAC	Media Access Control
NAT	Network Address Translation
NIST	National Institute of Standards and Technology
OMB	Office of Management and Budget
OS	Operating System
PC	Personal Computer
PDA	Personal Digital Assistant
PII	Personally Identifiable Information
PIN	Personal Identification Number
SMTP	Simple Mail Transfer Protocol
SSID	Service Set Identifier
SSL	Secure Sockets Layer
TKIP	Temporal Key Integrity Protocol
VoIP	Voice over Internet Protocol
VPN	Virtual Private Network
WEP	Wired Equivalent Privacy
WPA	Wi-Fi Protected Access
WPAN	Wireless Personal Area Network

Appendix D—Resources

The lists below provide examples of resources that might be helpful in securing devices used for telework.

Resource Sites

Site Name	URL
Home Computer Security	http://www.us-cert.gov/reading_room/HomeComputerSecurity/
Information for New and Home Users	http://www.cert.org/homeusers/
Interagency Telework Site	http://www.telework.gov/
NIST Security Configuration Checklists Program for IT Products	http://checklists.nist.gov/
Security at Home	http://www.microsoft.com/protect/default.mspx
Stay Safe Online	http://www.staysafeonline.info/

Documents

Document Title	URL
NIST SP 800-48 Revision 1, *Wireless Network Security for IEEE 802.11a/b/g and Bluetooth*	http://csrc.nist.gov/publications/PubsSPs.html
NIST SP 800-69, *Guidance for Securing Microsoft Windows XP Home Edition*	http://csrc.nist.gov/itsec/guidance_WinXP_Home.html
Safe at Any Speed	http://www.staysafeonline.org/basics/resources/FTCsafeatanyspeed.pdf
Seven Simple Computer Security Tips for Small Businesses and Home Computer Users	http://www.infragard.net/library/seven_tips.htm

Appendix E—Index

A

Administrative accounts, 5-2, B-1
Antispyware software, 5-5, 5-12
Antivirus software, 5-5, 5-12, 6-1
Application configuration, 5-8, 6-2
Attacks, 5-4
Authentication, 2-2, 3-2, 5-4, 6-1

B

Backups, 3-1
Bayesian spam filter, 5-7
Blacklist, 5-7, B-1
Bluetooth, A-2
Broadband router, 4-1

C

Cell phones, 6-1
Consumer device security, 6-1
Consumer devices, 2-2, B-1
Content filtering, 5-7, B-1
Cookies, 5-9, B-1

D

Daily use accounts, 5-2, B-1
Disinfect, B-1
Disk scrubbing, A-2
Downloading software, 6-2

E

Email clients, 5-10
Encryption, 2-2
Erasing information, 3-2
External networks, 4-4

F

File encryption, 3-1
Firewall appliance, 4-1

H

Home networks, 4-1
   Wired, 4-1
   Wireless, 4-2

I

Individual application access, 2-2
Infrared, A-2
Instant messaging clients, 5-11
Internet access methods, 2-2

Internet Protocol Security (IPsec), 2-1
Internet service provider (ISP), 4-1

L

Limited user accounts, 5-2
Loss or theft of device, 2-3

M

Macros, 5-11
Malicious code, B-1, *See* "Malware"
Malware, 2-3, 5-5, B-1
Media access control (MAC) address, 4-3
Mobile code, 5-10
Modem pools, 2-2

N

Networking, 6-1
Networking configuration, 5-3
Networking features, 5-3

O

Office productivity suites, 5-11
Organization devices, 2-3

P

Password, 6-1
Passwords, 5-2, 5-9, 5-12
Patches, 6-2
PC security, 5-1
Personal computers (PC), 2-2, B-1
Personal digital assistants (PDA), 6-1
Personal firewall, 4-1, 5-6, 6-1, B-1
Personal identification number (PIN), A-2
Personal information, 5-11
Personally identifiable information (PII), 3-1
Phishing, 5-9, B-1
Phone service security, A-1
Physical access, 5-3
Physical security, 3-1
Plug-in. *See* "Web browser plug-in"
Popup windows, 5-9, B-1

Q

Quarantine, B-1

R

Remote access, 2-1, B-1
Remote access software, 5-11
Remote access utilities, 5-4
Remote desktop, 2-1

www.ingramcontent.com/pod-product-compliance
Lightning Source LLC
Chambersburg PA
CBHW082113070326
40689CB00052B/4664